Bala Kids
An imprint of Shambhala Publications, Inc.
2129 13th Street
Boulder, Colorado 80302
www.shambhala.com

Cover art by Erin Huybrechts
Design by Kara Plikaitis

9 8 7 6 5 4 3 2 1

First Edition
Printed in China

Shambhala Publications makes every effort to print on acid-free, recycled paper.
Bala Kids is distributed worldwide by Penguin Random House, Inc.,
and its subsidiaries.

Library of Congress Cataloging-in-Publication Data
Names: Dodd, Carol, author. | Huybrechts, Erin, illustrator.
Title: Everything changes: and that's ok / Carol Dodd;
illustrated by Erin Huybrechts.
Description: First edition. | Boulder, Colorado: Shambhala, [2022]
Identifiers: LCCN 2020042621 | ISBN 9781611809299 (board)
Subjects: LCSH: Change—Juvenile literature.
Classification: LCC BD373 .D63 2021 | DDC 294.3/42—dc23
LC record available at https://lccn.loc.gov/2020042621

EVERYTHING CHANGES

AND THAT'S OK

Carol Dodd

illustrated by Erin Huybrechts

bala kids

Rain falls from clouds in the sky.
The sun appears, making everything dry.
Raindrops caught in a sunny beam,
a rainbow shimmers, like in a dream.

The moon is full, but then it's gone,
chased away by the dawn.

Stars that shine all through the night
disappear in morning's light.

EVERYTHING CHANGES, night to day.

EVERYTHING CHANGES, and that's OK.

We eat an apple, then plant the seeds,
water carefully, pull up the weeds.
A tree grows tall and strong.
Shiny new apples appear before long.

A yellow dandelion flower
slowly withers, hour by hour,
becoming fluffy seeds of white,
finally floating out of sight.

EVERYTHING CHANGES, day to night.

EVERYTHING CHANGES, and that's all right.

A kitten who loves to chase and scrounge becomes a cat who lives to lounge.

A puppy who only wants to play
grows into a dog who sleeps all day.

We read a book and turn each page,
learn more each day as we age.
Black hair slowly turns to gray.
Wrinkles come that won't go away.

EVERYTHING CHANGES—this is true.

EVERYTHING CHANGES, even you.

A new school might feel real strange.
Friendships sometimes rearrange.
Your best friend may move away,
but new friends will come to stay.

You build a sandcastle all day,
then a wave washes it away.
Your favorite game becomes a bore.
You don't want to play it anymore.

EVERYTHING CHANGES—it's the natural way.

EVERYTHING CHANGES, and that's OK.

You might feel sad
for quite a while,
then something happens
to make you smile.

You feel embarrassed
and close your eyes,
but then confidence returns,
a nice surprise.

Morning comes with the yellow sun.
The hours pass, and the day is done.
EVERYTHING CHANGES, day to night.
EVERYTHING CHANGES, and that's all right.

Stars shine brightly, sharp and clear,
then fade away when morning's near.
EVERYTHING CHANGES, night to day.
EVERYTHING CHANGES, and that's OK.

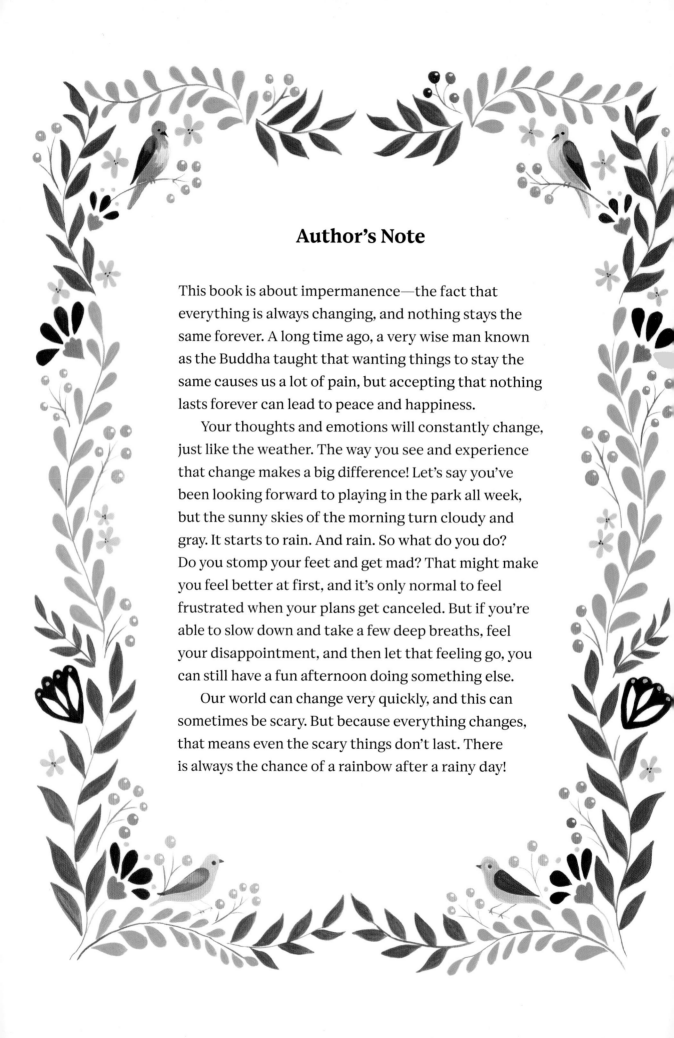

Author's Note

This book is about impermanence—the fact that everything is always changing, and nothing stays the same forever. A long time ago, a very wise man known as the Buddha taught that wanting things to stay the same causes us a lot of pain, but accepting that nothing lasts forever can lead to peace and happiness.

Your thoughts and emotions will constantly change, just like the weather. The way you see and experience that change makes a big difference! Let's say you've been looking forward to playing in the park all week, but the sunny skies of the morning turn cloudy and gray. It starts to rain. And rain. So what do you do? Do you stomp your feet and get mad? That might make you feel better at first, and it's only normal to feel frustrated when your plans get canceled. But if you're able to slow down and take a few deep breaths, feel your disappointment, and then let that feeling go, you can still have a fun afternoon doing something else.

Our world can change very quickly, and this can sometimes be scary. But because everything changes, that means even the scary things don't last. There is always the chance of a rainbow after a rainy day!